AERIAL

Also by Bin Ramke

The Difference between Night and Day

White Monkeys

The Language Student

The Erotic Light of Gardens

Massacre of the Innocents

Wake

Airs, Waters, Places

Matter

Tendril

Theory of Mind: New & Selected Poems

AERIAL

BIN RAMKE

OMNIDAWN PUBLISHING
RICHMOND, CALIFORNIA
2012

Cover art by Jan Aronson,
"Cloud Triptych #42"

Book cover and interior design by Cassandra Smith

Omnidawn Publishing is committed to preserving ancient
forests and natural resources. We elected to print this title on
30% postconsumer recycled paper, processed chlorine-free. As
a result, for this printing, we have saved:

4 Trees (40' tall and 6-8" diameter)
1,589 Gallons of Wastewater
1 million BTUs of Total Energy
101 Pounds of Solid Waste
352 Pounds of Greenhouse Gases

Omnidawn Publishing made this paper choice because our
printer, Thomson-Shore, Inc., is a member of Green Press
Initiative, a nonprofit program dedicated to supporting authors,
publishers, and suppliers in their efforts to reduce their use of
fiber obtained from endangered forests.

For more information, visit www.greenpressinitiative.org

Environmental impact estimates were made using the Environmental Defense
Paper Calculator. For more information visit: www.edf.org/papercalculator

Library of Congress Cataloging-in-Publication Data

Ramke, Bin, 1947-
Aerial / Bin Ramke.
    p. cm.
ISBN 978-1-890650-60-5 (trade pbk. : alk. paper)
I. Title.
PS3568.A446A684 2012
811'.54--dc23
                    2011051410

Published by Omnidawn Publishing, Richmond, California
www.omnidawn.com   (510) 237-5472   (800) 792-4957
10 9 8 7 6 5 4 3 2 1
ISBN: 978-1-890650-60-5

to Linda, Nic, Mary, Rick, Julie

We are edged with mist. We mark an unsubstantial territory.

Virginia Woolf, *The Waves*

CONTENTS

Clouded

Cloudless

CLOUDED

When ye see a cloud rise out of the west, straightway ye say,
There cometh a shower; and so it is

Luke 12:54

MIGRATIONS OF BIRDS AND FISHES

Nocturnal warnings fill us with desire
to know the arts of the birds
and the habits of fishes.
Our city, inhabited by shadows
of the migrants, feathery birds above
and below the river surface scaly
fish pass through darkly as we wave
at our windows, we sleepless
and full of fragments, dreams
and dreadful plans for tomorrow.
The land is the land, and home.
The water is the water, and home.
The light is the light is the air
and is its own home, we think.

What a contrite species this is
which does its damage by day and
by night regrets and dreams
or watches at windows.

LIVING IN WEATHER

It is an economy unfolding
of leaf of leaves into trees leaving of winter
and agonies of spring; fold and unfold

reading and reading leaves leaves
the mind implicated in its body, world:
it thinks, wild the epigraphy:

they shall beat their coins into cookware

pennies flattened serve roof repair

otherwise wilderness catches calligraphy

snares a bitter mind among mountains.
The loud clouds come falling
from air from the mountains.

Falling air and fair weathers
wash us of our sins any season.
Here how it happens — a measure:

the beetle imago crawling two
dots on its back shiny as dew
under the murderous eye of sun
I of sunlight sizzling the morning as

if and we wait again against. For health.

THESEUS AND THE YOUTH OF ATHENS

So write, tease
as you see fit, or
sew right ease, or
listen more carefully
as such language unfolds
itself before you, around unrolls

sorites, a word from
a word that means "heap."

The cloud began invisibly I assumed
molecules massing, a brain-shape forming
in my brain I watched the sharp horizon
beyond which the world ended from
which clouds arrive: when

when it becomes a heap, a bunch
as in, when does a group of molecules
gather itself sufficient volume and visibility
to become a cloud if water; a swarm if bees...

a game of words a gang of words into a
conversation or monologue or epic a bunch of
words willing itself into translation. Plutarch's

Vita Thesei, 22-23: "The ship wherein Theseus and
the youth of Athens returned had thirty oars, and was
preserved by the Athenians down even to the time of
Demetrius Phalereus, for they took away the old
planks as they decayed, putting in newer and stronger

timber in their place, insomuch that this ship became
a standing example among the philosophers, for the

logical question of things that grow; one side holding
that the ship remained the same, and the other
contending that it was not the same."

Boundary, bound, from Latin *bombus*, humming.
A sound, a sound bounded.

I was a child and you were a child we entered
from a chrysalis form reformed —
objects littering an apparentness of sky.
A breathing together a constancy.

EXPLICIT AT THE BEDSIDE

1

To maneuver calamity calmly
a boat moored to the window continued
(*yet she did suffer, not dream, in her bed*
was cared for but yet did die)

another escape — a walk through a maze not
thinking it a maze at the time at the time
a neuronal range of baffles — no
knowing why until a final turn and a tall
wall with a tall door and some voice or
writing named a noun and opened a door

to severe landscape unpopular "...a substance
growing on hills in the East, candied by the sun,
and of diverse colours" wrote Christopher Smart
and offered wishes numbering three I had
none beyond three childlike as

a well-known dilemma I lost count
near two, counting heavily against
mourners, watchers at death beds,

2

those who live among weathers the clouds
loudly proclaim familiar decline, a line
or border a breathing of boundaries away

engagements, engorgements, air and vapors;
who wouldn't wish a pristine inheritance
full already when we took possession air
and water and rock ready-made and yet
it brought me to this bedside besides to
count breaths counting down counting on
but this was my dream of water at the window
sill the slightest wave would wash over into
my room no room remaining a maze of rooms

a new skill developed a various hope a
discovery: a paper in a pocket, your mother's,
numbers unreadable possibly telephone
possibly proof of a small theorem overlooked
by all who came before, a conjecture turned
real, her proof; if I had been given those

3

wishes three wisely held closely passed on.
Whether the butterfly is happier than the
caterpillar because it is more beautiful, whether
the child is happier than the mother because
still alive still whether I spoke
to her in that manner or not
would she hear? She did not answer.
Care is a bondage, bond "The air
was tiny. / The air
would not do."   Anne Sexton

A narrow strip of cloud to clot the sunlight
cloud the afternoon, protect the one
who suffers.   I did Lie
next to her in her sickbed careless. A winding
down this modernly; first the pillow
then the body cools. "Here ends" or
abbreviation of *explicitus est liber*, the small
scroll unrolled no distinction between
unfolding unrolling, misfolded, (prion).
Clean sheets neatly stacked on the bed.
When I returned.

for Melba Guidry Ramke, 1917-2006

CLOUD CONTINUED

I asked my brother is it possible
to stand on a cloud, he said no. I said,
if we flew in an airplane into a cloud,
and I could open the window, could I
take a piece of the cloud,
maybe put it in my pocket? He said,
your pocket would get wet,
you would have nothing but a wet
spot on your shirt
when the plane landed.

I did maybe about that same time
consider keeping snow in the freezer.
Snow was a part of a cloud fallen,
as was rain, as was a wet
shirt forgotten on the line
as a thunderstorm performed.
Though I had not then seen snow.

IF SURFACE IS A VERB

Brown Pelicans watch loudly
cloudy crystals and a thinning future which
anyone could read: an ocean. It had a name.
Called home. Call it home. Like a dog, for instance
in the late evening called, the evenness ending;

ocean and its clouds — a small
dirty ocean like a Mediterranean but warmer
— Gulf of Mexico — The Gulf
the gray surface we lived on

from the Greek, κο'λπος "bosom," hence, "bay, gulf"
(= Latin *sinus*), and "hollow of the waves,
depth of the sea" when I call these things
to me, when I recall things; what you
call the present progressive
means times linger

(the Exxon Valdez, repaired and renamed
the Sea River Mediterranean, sails the Atlantic
and is prohibited by Alaskan law from returning
to Prince William Sound)

names can have a tense, you know — nouns
such as my soon-to-be-home in the future
tense. Tension, sounds like clouds,

≈

the timing of the growth of the breast — happens
rapidly — the timing of growth *within* — tumor, benign
or, and the rapidity with which breasts appear
a marker of adolescence,
or the tumor appears equally within

Breast, wave, fold. *Wave, particle, light,* J-L Nancy
the goddess within, against
a virgin Mary's unused parts
the breasts appear at the behest
of hormones, protein properly folded
hands in prayer, like linen waiting

or do they *surface*, verb, a fold
of flesh arising rising wavelike
approaching shore foam-tipped falling
a sci-fi love affair; rare again origami
fold enfold folio

such as a boy on the beach reading
his little book but looking across
waves at clouds clouding of the horizon
graves grays where gods might reveal

and sisters scattered along
sand strewn the beach delivered
of new obscurities, shapes engaging
him newly his present tense.
A shape the present takes, clouded
cup enfolded.

> (*"bosom," could, like "fathom," mean*
> *the space embraced between two arms*)

CRYSTALLINE STRUCTURE, THREAT OF WEATHER

Thomas Hopkins Gallaudet, founder
of the first American school for
the deaf, Wallace Stevens, and Samuel
Colt all 3 buried in Cedar Hill
Cemetery, Hartford, Connecticut.

Everything is necessary, nothing
is sufficient. Speak to see
who listens.

A manner of speaking as necessary attribute,
ubiquitous, annunciatory as bells, a rollicking
of winter air. Who speaks
still dies, eventually, if recent

events are any guide. I am silent standing
hat in hand and watching the spadesful flung
onto caskets, a tear here and there a hand wrung

while graying clouds dissipate, dilapidate and
dutiful humans homeward heading. We borrowed
the word from the Norse, *die*, but everyone always
had such a word, surely. If words were sure.

Here's a threat, of snow and eventually fallen
it will cover and convert the landscape; the littering
beneath the landscape the litter of us recent
dead decaying fallen as is our state — late
lamented living lying there a layer ghostly beneath
the blooming sod. Sad or funny? Funny. Funereal.
They dissipate, hissing; hear the sun strike each flake.

RECOVERY, TO COVER AGAIN

A breakable world made
manifest fracture a sight such as
globular clusters constructions
in which a one to one correspondence
between a set and some fragment
of that set is established
the correspondence defined by
rotations (isometries) and finite partitions
paradoxical decompositions
Felix Hausdorff proved a
paradox involving deformation
through various dimensions allowing
a single sphere to reform into two
complete spheres. Like clouds, say:
see how that one thins into two...
the vaporous vernacular of cloud...
the mind is that shape — no, the
brain. A surface electrical.

Paradox and *Paradise* as twins
of the same etymon, intimates:
imagine a cloud and then imagine it
inside itself, filling itself with self.

AERIAL

Flakes of air into words
distill along a wire;
from the shape of an aerial
my brother could read all kinds
of information forming;

it seemed a sort of spying.
It seemed to make a thing, matter:

every roof and radio
a writing writ by a god
in whose hand his breath was.

THE RESURGENCE OF PELICAN

A bird thought to kill her young out of anger
but to resurrect them by bleeding, "that is,
by confession out of the mouth that she sinned with
she should draw blood of sin out of her breast"
Ancrene Wisse, and other authorities
on such matters say that the Pelican feeds
her brood her blood abounding

but every bird builds a nest, some mid air
held aloft only by will and beating of wings
constant below, the wing exerts such pressure
on Air that Air is frightened to allow a thing
to fall through, any cloud of sticks and feathers,
such is the fearful trembling nature of Air,
which the blood overrules in his heat,

the heart a source of blood and of anger
for Pelican who loves her young and kills
through anger the bleeding the bleeding
beyond anger the birds of the air all
bleed a kind of knowledge or courage.

IMAGO

Nothing isolate, all are pulled
by and pulling upon all, the waters
internal, blood of many colors
(gravity makes shapes
of us, skin over fluid)

to feel with the eye
of water welling, tear, like
a well or wall of water to feel, full
as it is itself, defined by fullness
like me or you among ourselves
wading...waiting

to shape of self and water
enclosed, is the enclosure — oh, a small
creature (ladybug) lyric within her
exoskeleton, a shape of self watery
dewy it is early

in the day her color close to
the color of poppy, the two dots of wing
coverings (there is a name for)
a summer symmetry, tenderly elytra

let a little water be fetched, and wash your feet,
and rest under a tree:

all the sleeps will resound with your own
slow breathing they regulate themselves
clocklike sounding a burden each sleeper
bundled into herself the Fairy Tale of
sleep protected by thorn-bushes and paralysis,
like gods patient and potent, like walls

(the beetle modified front wings into protective
coverings, the fly modified back wings into
club-shaped halteres, gyroscopic; Ovidian).

INTO BAD WEATHER BOUNDING

(After Wallace Stevens' "Of The Surface Of Things")

Colligated points, dust, ultimately a cloud, as in
an orographic cloud in Colorado cringing against
a horizon. Boundaried vision and vapor conspire

to exhale, exalt into rain random dispersal into
the present: I see as far as that. I never saw farther.

In sinking air, mammatus cloud a sign the storm
has passed is passing...I walk happily whenever
or sometimes pass the last bad sign the bounded

land, I am sad as you are doubtless. Sad said
the bad man, somber. Otherwise say:
In my room the world is beyond
my understanding; / But when I walk I see
that it consists of three or four hills
and a cloud.

CONTRADICTION, AND THE ENIGMATIC MODES

     also silence might also be
white noise — all frequencies all intensities all
distance as an imagined reciprocal of absence

                    we never say what we mean but
we try we fill in the blanks of what we leave/
discover in the left over silence. Maybe Wittgenstein
never said this.
                    When my brother died I felt
a new fear. This selfish response was a strange
reciprocal. I felt him as absence. But then what I
felt, (I did feel), could not have been absence
but new presence. Our last visit involved
an hour watching Kodak slides of our past
projected onto a sheet pinned to his living room wall.
(His rented hospital bed wouldn't fit in his bedroom,
and besides, in those last days he chose the social
at last, the presence of the still living). The sheet's
whiteness opened itself to the presence of a past,
the lyric light. We had, his wife and I, looked
through the basement for the official screen,
the rolled-up beaded version, but we
failed. We made do.

To refer to light as lyric is a fanciful gesture.
We were photographers; he was skilled and
deeply technically proficient. My own work
clumsy in all the public ways, but out of sight
I was better. I became a darkroom technician,
spent nights locked in a bathroom breathing
noxious fumes, peering into pans of fixer,
developer, short-stop, under romantic
red light (these were the days of silver

halides and safe lights). There were light-leaks
to worry me, pinholes in the bellows,
the enlarger covered with tape, a towel
against the door to keep out sunrise, which
would surely come again. And all that absence
contained, containing, molecular memory
on the treated surface of film and paper. The
lyre was a simple instrument plucked
to produce a tune to sing to, to
say words against.

FACTORIZATION VS HERALDRY

1 The facts of my life are paltry, pale, forgotten

2 did you know that "erase" a term from heraldry referred to the
jagged outline of an animal's head

3 or maybe it meant "uproot" related to "radical"

4 Boethius: My Griefs have dulled my memory, and eras'd almost
everything out of it

5 the coefficient was invented (or discovered) late
in the history of mathematics — a sort of
second unknown, not an x but an a

6 the effect of information is to obliterate the memory

7 to infect

8 I used to love numbering segments of poems, making
a larger entity of hurried fragments

9 this would result in momentum, cause me to move
forward anticipating pleasures of completion plus
the excitement of beginning

10 over

11 I could feel those pleasures dozens of times in an afternoon
rather than waiting weeks at a stretch for completion of some

12 long project that in the end no one including me
remembered the reasoning behind

13 the Wyvern, a two-legged dragon, if *proper* it is green
with a red chest, belly, and underwings

14 *incensed* means with flames issuing forth from mouth and ears

15 the manufacture of facts is the poem, a life.

REMINDED

Mingling over the years growing
vinelike into vascular awareness, an

arrangement of anxieties into what
we will call *Mind.*

To mind is to care. Or object.
Or attend to. Verbs are best.

It was the era when all
young humans thought alike and opposed

the opposition. We read the papers.
Sunlight intruded,

ordinary warmth as a virtue,
virtual adversary, astral. We said:

Be afraid of things that can name you:
the search for Eden is fear of a future.

All appalling after night the morning
comes and sleep was a mourning

it wiped away the skyfull of asterisks.
"Als das Kind Kind war"   Peter Handke

When the child was a child there were
fig trees lining the lawn, beyond

was a wood, thick with weeds, wilderness
to a human child — always music mingled

coming across the weeds, and after rain
fish appeared in every puddle;

or here was weather in the house
and we lived that way forever during

childhood; some
times it was snow that would fall

through such ceilings,
and sometimes rain.

He bindeth up the waters in his thick clouds; and the cloud is not rent under them.

Job 26:8

MINDED

Sunlight intrudes one late afternoon;
although ordinarily welcome
to the reader an arrogant adversary,
ordinary, a problem...

I am afraid of all things I can name.
Eden: a steady-state ecosystem without history;
birdsong as necessity, not diversion;
any kind of greenness dies when
you look too close —

the bark of the tree
the roots and leaves and birds

at night when sky is full of asterisks, like
mind! arising full of warning.

TO BREATHE TOGETHER

the breathing of humans and animals, a stone falling
in Europe or America, the light of a fire and of the sun
  Newton's "Principle of Homogeneity" exemplified.

One memory is of her pinning   One memory is of her
clothes to a line, the light   clothes, light and
and the heat a conspiracy   heat her conspiracy

"You look into someone's eyes as if you were seeing
through the face" Mei-mei Berssenbrugge
wrote once but whether in praise or horror—
tremble of the surface
of the water in the well of the eyes—all
are (are all?) engaged.

The bird-bath encrusts itself, crystalline
graph, birds huddle and I watch from the window
the glazing of water. The cortex is all surface
except that the color of light is inconstant
and the glittered awareness shines through
too many layers to tell any sort of tenderness.
Like rough bark of the tree touching.
Is it, it is possible to love this which died
in such a past as that. All tendencies coalesce;
all surface is true and troubled. Her washing,
the mother's in that era, hung in the sun its light
a helpmeet and she was a vision, envisioned.

CONTINUOUS COMPUTATION
(1 THROUGH 3)

1

Middleton Manigault

To cure him of his mind is to unstir
the egg from the batter; who
is he but embodied mind:

follow like a detective the
privacy of I, of eye, follow
like a road not like a road

but the road a following a flowing
the old lost road through the woods...
But there is no road through the woods.   Kipling

To care to cure him of his own
mind a road through a yellow wood
strewn with webs, spiderly work wise

through the night mindful of morning
to come, the flies to come buzzing
Om Mani Padme Hum the spider says

while weaving to feel not hear
the sonorous vibrating self the
spider can not speak for she has

no mouth for breathing only for feeding
nor mind never — the morning mind
of earth-filled Earth with webs glisten
and lovely, love is mind even
in its illness, odd, stillness divided even
not diminished, dimmed. Dear.

2

Colour is lyght incorporate in a body visyble pure & clene.
                                          Giles Du Wes

Yesterday a rainbow, a hundred degrees of arc but
the varying intensity still a kind of wholeness, a reminder:
color has been much on his mind these recent days,
momentous days, and his hunger, too, tends toward
a circular shape, a circulation between body and visible
air, tangible, particles of sun and dust and water...

by "his" I meant "my" and yet not, also: there are forms
of life which can be touched like rain, falling, and other
forms which can be seen or simulated, color, named
and ordered (Newton's distinction,
                              "indigo" from "violet.")
When the rainbow is doubled it is a mirroring, reversed
order of color; maybe I saw the second one, maybe not.

Hovering. The word has a vibrating quality, like bees
above blossoms. Color to engulf. Threaten.

3

Monstrous Silhouette

A pear tree's leaves lost evenly —
each limb has a remaining dozen
or so; a single bird appearing

41

anxious, peering — her shape mimics
leaves even if her movement does not.
If her quick movement brings cold wind.
If her bright eye brings snow.
If then she breathes a kind of patience.

1

Arguing with Water, Welling

This well or wall of water I feel, full
as it is of itself, defined itself by fullness
like me or you among ourselves wading...

let a little water be fetched, and wash your feet,
and rest under a tree.

Nothing stands isolate, all are pulled by and pulling
upon all. The secret human hatreds, he said

to nobody, everybody hurrying past anxious
to get home anxious to respond
to the attractive spouse or mother or the pet
sitting on the other side of the door waiting
hoping feeling the miles and years dissolve
by a factor of the distance yet to be squared,
thinness of the door notwithstanding.

All the sleeps will resound with your own
slow breathing they will regulate themselves
clocklike sounding a burden each sleeper

bundled into herself the Fairy Tale of
sleep protected by thorn-bushes and paralysis,
like gods patient and potent, like walls
، of water welling tear-like.

2

Spin

Kevon Johnson on the Brooklyn Empire
skating rink closure: *...we skate counter-clockwise,*
which means we skate against time. We stay young.

What spins inspires, breathes into

as in: every thing is attracted to every
other. This is the formula to measure
how much: multiply the masses, divide
by the square of their distance apart.

Unstable as water, thou shalt not excel.

3

The Movies

She negotiates exits to exist this way
that way to the world made of light
watery as it looks from here if it is night
you might as well

stare through the screen wall
into the world which is locally dark.

Stars a moon or two. To speak to stay
the screen's voice calls
for the attention of the living, leaving
though she may be sleeping, sleepy
especially if black and white as
the checkerboard squared floor
she dances across acrostically
alive lithe dancing. Spinning

past her is a past

just this side of the exit sign sighing
us out.

1

White Russian

In a cocktail short glass add ice, add the vodka, then
the kahlua, then the cream. Serve unstirred.

2

Such a Thing Comes from Such a Thing

und dass so was von so was kommt   Carlo Karges

What was thought to be Thought turns out to be Thing;

so speaking among ourselves we rarely listen.
In the corner one hums, unhurried.

There are those who can hum anything
to anyone, and to make love this way is to make
with the mouth an apocalypse of purpose;
the teeth remain covered, the hard
edge to the mouth mysterious,
remains momentous memory.

Love as made is not a thing. Or is thought.

3

Offering a Gift Fig, a Finer Fog

"Suffering, if taken seriously, serves

a purpose" (wrong, if true).
Fog if torn by sound into increments
substitutes for weather; breeding, if torn
into terror, engages every mind minded — sever
hope from happiness, she said, laughingly.

She was his therapist, a gift the world
offered: "I keep no rank nor station.
Cured, I am frizzled, stale and small" Lowell
later wrote, lettering his littered mind
to art, we claim. She calmed him
all concerned, convinced, and failing.

The fig is emblem of several things: gift
of gathered interiors, a small bower
for wasps: did she know that "gift" old
enough once meant payment for a wife?
Who didn't, in her bones. The plural for wedding.

Or the German for poison. Strong feminine.

Interesting terrible facts are rifts

or gifts as of a nesting tier of wasps
or all the greens I tint imaginatively
of any small, cured, stale imagined man,

and yet those wasps do hover, of all the hymenoptera,
over the notion of bowering bliss, of gift, of bed:
agaonidae, wasps which insert themselves
into the inflorescence (syconium) to breed—
o touch, o careless. Like love, such gifted agony.

1

A Universe of Discourse, Objects to Which Variables Refer

"The trouble is that I cannot drink a single glass of water,
though the craving itself is some satisfaction"

Although Kafka wrote such a thing beyond speaking—
the voice destroyed by disease, a symptom shared
by many, my mother for instance, and Freud—
there was a speech of desire in the deathbed

a conversant body building its energy resonantly
as crystal at the dinner table, the wetted finger
rounding and rounding, ringing.

The voice has no surface but

His voice failed him and us; voice is mind
departing continually dissipating soul-like a long
death in its way it began with the first word it
is mere vibration — Raynaud's disease by other name —
...what is that curve called which is
given by the inverse of the radius
of the osculating circle? To kiss

is not to ask, to not ask but
to desire and be silent.

2

Manigault Reconsidered

Did he see what he wanted was it
worth hungering that much
he believed starvation —
stare into the rigid moment
like the past like the future —
some starlike quality of mind
induced by body produced
in him a state of intense seeing
and the death was accidental.
Ah well. His silence, his desire —
the crude implication, to be rigid
with desire or rigor.

3

...to imagine that which we know   Shelley

To long for is to pine, is to punish.
No, to reach toward, to yearn, to bravely wail.

The language he could speak was finical,
more accurate than any hearer could imagine.
To know is enough, never enough too
much knowing involutes, involves, for instance

an osculating circle whose sine, written sin,
engages the variant universe at one spot,
one little point only, how lovely:

our calculations have outrun conception;

we have eaten more than we can digest. Then starve
a self into submission, as they did:
Manigault, Weil, Gödel, Clarke, Sands, Thileepan...

... enlarges the circumference of the imagination
by replenishing it with thoughts of ever new delight,
which have the power of attracting and assimilating
to their own nature all other thoughts and which
form new intervals and interstices
whose void forever craves fresh food.

DESIRE. CONSIDER. STAR. ICE.

An astronomy—asterisked self
as lover: some constellation,
consolation: there a maiden enchained,
there a hunter's desiring
to kill every animal there is
Orion, belted by Betelgeuse, pulsing;

≈

Better the actual star, isolate,
distance and time the measure
to be: (space) an ice cube glittering
a nice glittering cube
I see an option an alter-
native to any original
concept. Desiderate,
better, better than ever.
I am thinking these days about
Time, and Space, and the Difference,

How sexual it is, the shapes of space,
timing of words; she knew me
better than anyone, a secret
option, the collection collated
systematic and sensual. Operation.
They sometimes wear stars on
their clothes and the machine connects
those dots, wire-frame photography
can make a cube of comfort—strength,
fortitude at its base, still in the

Old French *espace* meant time,

but *shape* was a word for sex,

49

the organ—original. Ordinal,

or ordinary,

this secretly separate sifting
of a self particulate, drifting

≈

like ice the elegant feel of it falling
into itself, above and below a self
formed crystalline, symmetric

slippery. They long, the little ones
abed, for the slippery touch tangling
self with self, earth with earth.

THERE WAS EVER ONLY ONE SANCTITY

(After Mary Oliver)

She said You have only to let
the soft animal of your body
love what it loves. Dear Mary
Other Mary: Mother Most Amiable,
Mother Most Admirable, Mother
of Good Counsel. And if you recall

the nights and can arrange for
a new light to come calling
crawling assuaging the curious
felt guilt of the soft body, then
do so, seriously felonious Self.

Tower of Ivory, Tower of David,
House of Gold were the names
of my pets at the time, they
loved me, soft-bodied things.

Morning Star, pray for me.
Mirror of Justice, Seat of Wisdom,
Comforter of the Afflicted,
Cause of Our Joy. *Build your own
cloud chamber dot com:*
the hardest part is the radioactive
sample — consider using an old
alarm clock with luminous dial, or
americium from a smoke detector
or tailings from an abandoned
pitchblende mine, or
uranium glass from the nineteenth
century; recall small deceptions
the small bells ringing off-stage,

the smell of burning. All recall
the night when she arranged
for new light to come calling
crawling to assuage the curious
felt guilts of a soft body that
dies so, did so seriously;
the body always darkest against
which the particles whiz
arrow-like hissing against
a soft dark background
for viewing lines
of cloud which did mark
where once was movement
now nothing, particles
love another as if god
could have a mother. Another.

CLOUD AS AN OPEN SET MAPS ONTO THE HILLSIDE

under which we do and did sit
smelling the clover
then plucked
a stem which we would knot and
interlace with
another stem forming
a chain of clover in simple knots
as each cloud
of clover blossom
desiccates it loses something life
some of us grew
tired of the game arose
and returned home green stains
on our clothes
were not a problem no one's
mother noticed that night before dinner.

Were we in any way under the cloud
or under
the shadow of the cloud
the angle of sunlight against us
sharpening as
evening progressed
what is *under* is it a vision?

WE WHO LIVE HERE SEE AIR

the shapes it takes in other air, clarity
partial potential

peaks often snow-covered the mountain
never its own color of air

over the air the dark of invisible
glitters

the shapes of air are many I collect
them all, my small hobby

here are approaches for
the nonlinear analysis of

for example
mountain air radiant

a study of cloud as boundary

geometric and equilibrial relations
in explicit closed forms

variations on cloud, condensate forming
its own skin — the edge of cloud

above a mountain-shaped mass
with snow which formed then fell through its own

cloud is one kind.

CIPHER

Privacy privileges an *inside*. We are social creatures we are
told. Words get out, outside, and when our mother began
her disease she knew the difference, inside *versus* outside.
Deprived, she spoke even when eating, when she could eat.
Then she could speak but not swallow so a hole was made in
her where food could go in. Then she could no longer speak
but when I visited she wrote things on a notebook she carried
with her always. Always I carried a notebook too but she could
hear so I did not write. She wrote but then her hands shook
and then she did not write and did not eat and did not leave
her house her room her bed and there is a kind of breathing
called Cheyne-Stokes which she did which was a sign the
boundary between inside and outside was growing firmer,
sharper and then the breathing stopped. Her last note I kept
I have been trying to decipher. I know some of the words.

...by day in a pillar of a cloud, to lead them the way; and by night in a pillar of fire, to give them light; to go by day and night

Exodus 13:21

FAIR WEATHER CUMULUS

have the appearance of floating cotton and have a lifetime of
5 to 40 minutes   www.2010.atmos.uic.edu

The evaporation of water at their edges
causes air to cool causes
air to be denser than other air thus

fall through other air separated by what
kind of boundary, what edge, what is
the difference between this air and that?

is an inappropriate question. The blue
is more intense than the grays and whites
within it but what is appearance

except appearance? *aeira, aerea, aeria, airea, area, aria,*
ayeria, ayrea, eyria, eiria, erea, eria (feminine)
aerius, erius, heyrius (masculine) and *ayerium* (neuter)

for the nest or brood of a bird of prey frequently
from 1086 in British sources; not to mention
aera, aira, eyra in continental sources

the falcon descended from such air
through like air, airily descending
wispy like cotton. Reaping.

AGAIN AGAINST. ENUMERATION

Whenever you can, count.
> Francis Galton

"All we can know is difference." No thing is
still and still enough, whatever ether it lives
in breathing — I am speaking of the minerals —
I defer to some significance
within and among the types. And every often so
we can measure degrees of. This is one,
a kind of poetry:

Imagine a child who does not live his life but
lives the parent's life, adheres to in-difference
to become only what was wanted. This bloom
this morning a light blue a litheness of color
a morning glory (doxology — praise imagines
sameness — was in the beginning etc. to end)
without end a kindness.

One may disagree about a system, an idea, a date,
a resemblance, but I do not see how anyone could
fail to accept the simple idea of enumerating.
> Apollinaire, *The Cubist Painters*, 1913

How can we tell the difference? Telling is a
word, a kind of counting. Toll. Tell the difference
between the black cloud and the gray, gray
being a code: Frank *Gray* (1887-1969), U.S.
physicist, *Gray code*, in which consecutive
integers represented by binary numbers
differ in only one

digit, published by him in 1947 U.S. Patent
2,632,058. Louis Harold Gray (1905-65),
English radio-biologist a unit of absorbed
dose of ionizing radiation, corresponds to
absorption of one joule of energy per
kilogram of absorbing material; 100 rads.
Symbol Gy. Or variant spellings

noted in the OED: "Many correspondents said
that they used the two forms with a difference
of meaning or application: the distinction most
generally recognized being that *grey* denotes a
more delicate or a lighter tint than *gray*. Others
considered the difference to be that *gray* is a
'warmer' colour, or

that it has a mixture of red or brown" dis-
tinction being the better part. The child does
his bit, his best, the glory.
Enumeration, the book of Numery, some
other way into the count engages him happily
as he draws his circles compassed and his
lines straight

a corpse is a continent anyway, full
of living things, enumerable, innumerable,
crawling so hard to count anyway. Within
and some without, as the child's rhyme
once told, late at night frightening. Color

is a kind of counting, of waves, say
or just the bright
exuberance of atoms bouncing bounded
while children make of the waxy world

a sun yellow a tree green a squirrel brown
an apple red a window blue a sky blue
a mother a father a brother a sister count
browns and pinks and mottled telling
a ghastlier conspiracy lives.

A MEASURED NARROWNESS

The hare's breath trembled the
leaf before the teeth devoured
narrowness of space between
hungers. Wretched rabbit.
A miniscule mind mattering
is a thing, is a smallness
of thing this lovely evening
when we sit on stones and
light creases the grasses before
us. Parkland. Seasons. A thing
called cognitive dysmetria applies
so every rabbit reduces — distinguish
hare from rabbit, light from
even lighter. Hispid Hare with
her little leverets bounding.
The leporid, or so
I imagine, is under this turf
with altricial babies, worrying.
What we call them,
Lagomorphs, part of the world.
Who says it, and why, and whether
"matter" means to make into
world what was only mind before:

orography, hill writing, makes clouds;
makes clouds rain. The little molecules
rabbitly rattling down the tin roof;
but the rabbits are safe in their holes
and the hares are faster than lightning,
and the writers all rigor and rightness.

NEPHELOMANCY

There is appearance, and there is appearance
and a loud cloud contains such sparks as any dog fears;
there is shade and there is shadow all the same;
there is shape and shape is destiny when distant.

"He will send down upon you the cloud, pouring
down abundance of rain, And help you with   *Sura 71, 11-12*
wealth and sons, and make for you gardens,
and make for you rivers."

And the nicest thing about a garden is the wall, the wisdom
of separation, neighbor from neighbor at night.
And thunder comes and with it the comfort of home.

"And it was said: *O earth, swallow down*   *Sura 11, 44*
your water and O cloud, clear away   Holy Qur'an
and the water was made to   Trans. M.H. Shakir
abate and the affair was decided"

A stillness within the cloud is contention
is forces momentarily equal — momentous from
childhood under protection, momentum,
a sort of umbrella, (umbrage)
two towering nations (born) leaned equal against
themselves — cold wars & old scars

instead of arks we built holes
and lined them with foodstuffs and water
in cans and lined them with lead and lingered
until the air cleared of poisons...that was the plan.

≈

62

The shape of the cloud was called *mushroom*.
Consider: toadstool-shaped cloud. Consider: smoke.
The shadowed forms on walls of men and women
the flesh itself flame.

≈

we sometimes see clouds quickly massing together
on high and marring the serene face of the
firmament while they caress   Lucretius
the air with their motion...   De Rerum Natura
they never cease to dissolve and change their shapes

Nephelomancy or Aeromancy *aeroskopia* (Greek
divination by observing the sky) Variant Forms, Middle
English: aermacye, aeromance, aeromancye,
aeromauncie, aerymancie. Early Modern English:
aeromancie, æromancy, aëromancy, aeromanty, eromancy,
heromanty. New Latin: aeromantia, aëromantia.

I look and see a lamb in shape
and color and mildness of an afternoon
and wafting into itself it sleeps a cloud
just as easily leonine in shape, in some
such lying mode, useful to know
one would suppose, or hope.

STRATAGEMS AND SPOILS

The new season is colder than the previous,
a normal course of events. We see breaths
before all the lovely humans this evening, each
a little huddled into himself, herself, none
saunter, all purposeful. Clouds lead them
and for a few minutes the sunlight angled
to brighten the breath and darken the faces.

A bright breath to all, to all a sweet dream.

SWEET AND VARIOUS

Let Jeduthun rejoice with the Woodlark, who is sweet and various
Christopher Smart

Having cut myself loose from,
having cut losses, a self lost, a little I
ventured into the new era; are ventures
ever new, about to happen era

Now I know in part; but then shall I know even as also I am known
St. Paul

or again, having freed myself
I found myself at loss, at loose
ends and tied therefore into knots
not only adventurous move-making

but freed ends of any knot are a loss
a little errant sense of non-knotty
issuance: "knot" being a three dimensional
enclosure of a two dimensional object,

strings tangle. I understand the brain
is a tangle of long threads (the nervy parts)
touching, contact electrical is a self
a severed

I am myself, true, but that's little
help to me of my young past who knew better
persons and knew it but still was different
from them. Perverse child, inverted

We present an extension of our earlier observations on
symmetries in operation in the weak decays of heavy mesons
containing a single heavy quark. The new symmetries allow us
to obtain absolutely normalized model-independent predic-

I too would once speak this way, wanted to
and felt my failure into poetry, failed away from
the new knowing and the clarity obtained

tions in the heavy quark limit of all of the form factors
for the $Q_1 \to Q_2$ induced weak pseudoscalar and
pseudoscalar to vector transitions in terms of a single
universal function $\xi(t)$ with $\xi(0) = 1$.
   Nathan Isgur and Mark B. Wise

I knew Nathan as a child, I a child and he a child
and the land was as usual at war with the sky
as we were learning to count the complications
and to spend the nights away from home, our homes.

Sentences inherit their meanings from
beliefs with which they are correlated

Let Zorobabel bless with the Wasp, who is the Lord's architect,
and buildeth his edifice in armour.

Nathan spoke kindly to me and I was younger
than anyone can imagine. Not a theory yet
knot theory holds that origami cannot answer

all questions, and yet I find such comfort in the unfolding,

the paper still paper, still there to become some other
shape and comfort:

Let P, P' be two points of the paper that are brought into
coincidence by the process of folding. Then any point A
of the crease is equidistant from P, P', since the lines AP,
AP' are pressed into coincidence. The crease, being the locus
of points A, is the perpendicular bisector of PP'

and then again how many folds into a crane
a symbol of longevity and luck and balance
obtains, and I fold and I fold until I must
make a choice: one end the head, the other tail,
and a tiny fold breaks symmetry

or look there a shadow on a hillside
in the shape of a living child's brain which is a sheet
of flesh folding into the inside of a cranial cavity
the shape of certain clouds, and like clouds contains
electricity dangerous and dimensionless.
But folded, unfolded, explicit.

LITERACY: BLINDING BIRDS

To speak in order to establish one's rightness is
to speak in order to silence the other
                                    Emmanuel Levinas

Watch birds sinuous slide against nitrogen
mixtures, airs above, clouds of bright birds
clouds bright of bird-clotted air

Snow angels, or the prints of wings in snow
and bits of blood, solitaries
who hunt at night

Also architecture
designed as if to kill birds away. Building
with glass. I am afraid I say to myself

Airs live and breed in flocks which
take hours to fly past a still point in Africa
a billion red-billed queleas the most numerous
of birds followed by a million a flock of arctic geese

thousands of sociable lapwings in Turkey

≈

Birds balloons and train wrecks she reported on
in her dream: I was walking along a railroad track
I looked up to see huge balloons falling
then a flock of birds landed on the balloons

And the balloons again began falling
then I was accompanied by a friend walking
along a railroad and the train jumped the track
and hit me but the birds were unhurt high higher

I dreamt I looked over to my left and into the distance
and saw birds (black) flying
in a sort of circular fashion. Quite a lot of them
and I felt fear. Today we went to look at used cars

when we were leaving my husband told me to look
over there and I looked left and
there they were the birds I saw in my dreams.
It was 4 pm (just going dark in the UK)
and it was exactly like my dream. I don't understand

who would; owls could be blind I suppose
and survive like bats. Maybe not. Glass
shines yet light passes through, glare
is when some shines through some bounces off.
In the snow I see that stutter of owl
wings dipped into the snow five times

As the mouse or vole or whatever flightless
mammal frightful ran

At first light the flocks leave their roost to go for water and
from a distance it looks as though a grass fire has started. The
queleas form into dense, highly synchronised flocks which
look like clouds of smoke, and then, as the flock approaches
you, the numbers are so vast their wing-beats sound like a high
wind. We have been fortunate enough to witness this spectacle
at Amboseli where we sat for ten minutes while a single flock of
queleas made their morning trip from the swamp to the grassland
to feed.   http://www.kenyabirds.org.uk/quelea.htm

69

≈

A turning, untuning:

only the clouds are more dangerous
than a tropical people

it is not a life it is a lingering
my self in sunlight in wet air
suffused with reflected photons

so green with banana leaf
with elephant-ear and when sound
bounces above our streets

it engages green, mildews
and mysteries of the ponds
we will re-fuse the bombs

a turning a turning like
poetry we will march slovenly
into their hearts full of chambers

we will refuse their offered peace
the refuse of mortalities

plover, Charadriidae, *pluvia*, rain

*Let Jael rejoice with the Plover, who whistles for his live, and foils the marksmen
and their guns.*   Wrote Christopher Smart (fragment B,l)

≈

A dream of Starlings —
the mind circles itself clouding the

70

light the flight of the circling creatures
— of air of dust borne into the light
sunset orange a slight

engagement and then gone
the vapors and birds mix eloquent
ganglia and molecules and photons
as if several communities

made a language a languor of flight
they do seem, clouds disgorging birds
into light and air, they do seem not
of my world but only of themselves

Socrates: *At the Egyptian city of Naucratis, there was*
a famous old god, whose name was Theuth; the bird
which is called the Ibis is sacred to him, and he was
the inventor of many arts, such as arithmetic and
calculation and geometry and astronomy and
draughts and dice, but his great discovery
was the use of letters.

ERASURE'S SURE ERA

Scraping away like the cricket at his own hind leg

they said, without size, sang, a chorus
Greekly. But one thin Erica twined
her heavy hair and languished, lovely.
A lover named Erica, I, am Erica.
A nation so-called

what name he gave her counted
against the amputation the pruning—

only the animals save us (from what?)
What salvation, salve, absolution, ablution
erase it

a lack of contrails in the blue sky
of Chicago the afternoon 11 September
two-thousand-and-one like art
like Erased DeKooning. I watched
               while waiting for a train
                       listened.

≈

At the piano Jue He has two hands, hurrah but
hear her use just one
then what to do with the right? Hold on tight.

Matuschka, beauty out of damage (1993).

If thy right eye offend thee, pluck it...between
Matthew and Mark they could not decide
if erasure allows entrance into this world or
that one, the kingdom of God with one eye,
or "enter into life with one eye" all to avoid
the body burning,
the pruned limb expended; salvage something.

≈

I conceive, King Gelon,
that among men who do not have experience of
mathematics, such a thing* might appear incredible.
On the other hand, those who know of such matters
and have thought about the distances and sizes
of the earth, the sun, the moon, and
the universe in its entirety will accept them
due to my argument, and that is why I believed
you might enjoy having it brought to your attention.
                    Archimedes, "The Sand Reckoner"

*How big the world is, is a thing, its size.

≈

Cricket's sawing movement does not cut
but such a scene it makes as if to free
itself from its own legs, saw-toothed
shape seems cutting

the sound is loved, lucky, fills a house
bereft with luck, happenstance. Luck and locks.

≈

She is a kind of orphan, was born that way
her mother explained. She has no dolls
or any token of her own childhood
her mother gave them all to missionaries,
to missionary children, orphans of god of goodness.
She is lovely and thin
and has small hands since little things only
fit there her hold is hidden.
She makes her way in this world. She cuts
her own hands away at the wrists, softly.

Scrape the surface darkly
erase the print the paint the ink graphite
Praise the one-armed
busyness cover the old rejected wall and praise
Maurice Ravel and Paul Wittgenstein
yes to Brahms and Bartók,

Janácek, Saint-Saëns, Prokofiev,
Scriabin, Strauss and all who found
ways to praise the body scattered and torn
healed smaller than before born

                    into erasure

Parts missing The prize the price is loss

did make a music of it

Crickets in cages could fight, tickled to attack
by golden prods, hair-thin

mission, admission—send, send to. sin.

I had suddenly a sense of how weird
it is that a child can speak of itself, can say
"I was born there" and with its own thin
finger point in some, possibly accurate,
direction. Of itself it speaks. How odd a destiny.
As the cloud is consumed and vanisheth   Job 7:9
away: so he that goeth down to the grave
shall come up no more.

Born, burn: "When light reflects off a curve then
the envelope of the reflected rays is a caustic
by reflection or a catacaustic. First studied
by Huygens and Tschirnhaus, 1678."
A cloud surrounds everything
and will clear a path
or the disappearance
the weather clears like a word
.

PROVERBIAL CATTLE

Till the Cows come home.

The great clouds of them crowd
fundamental and assured of their doom
and ours; patient like all patience a
product of ignorance — abandoned
fields smoky in the morning — mist will rise in sun
light and heat while birds wander picking
at seeds in the drying dung; cows consume.

Cows consume great masses of grass: this
is no news;
Chaucer wrote: God sendeth a shrewd cow a short horne.
Shakespeare wrote it again later.

A cow may catch a hare, but not often

A poor man's cow dies, a rich man's child

An ill cow may have a good calf

As comely as a cow in a cage

As cows come to town : some good, some bad

As mad as the baiting bull of Stamford:

R. Butcher, in his Survey of Stamford, page 40: *William, Earl
Warren, lord of this town in the time of King John, standing
upon the castle walls of Stamford, saw two bulls fighting for a cow
in the meadow, till all the butcher's dogs, great and small,
pursued one of the bulls (being maddened with noise and multitude)
clean through the town. This fight so pleased the said Earl,
that he gave all those meadows (called the Castle Meadows),
where first the bull duel began, for a common to the butchers
of the town (after the first grass was eaten), on condition they*

find a mad bull, the day six weeks before Christmas Day,
for the continuance of that sport every year.

Barley straw's good fodder when the cow gives water

Many a good cow hath an evil calf

The cow gives good milk, but kicks over the pail

Set a fool to roast eggs, and a wise man to eat them
Set a herring to catch a whale, or a sprat to catch a herring
Set a cow to catch a hare

Take a man by his word, and a cow by her horns

The cow knows not what her tail is worth till she has lost it

The cow little giveth, / that hardly liveth

The cow that's first up gets the first o' the dew

The cow with the iron tail...

I always fear all things I love
especially horned cattle; such eyes
turn toward me as cows raise
their mouths from grazing; it did not

occur to me there was air
between us, all of us breathe air
all of us lobe-lunged are literate of air;
they wear themselves eagerly as I
wear sweaters, they wear shoes of horn

What should a cow do with a nutmeg?

You may beat a horse till he be sad, and a cow till she be mad

A head of cattle, head of head, cattle of cattle. Capital

Cap, cape, chapel. Cope. Capitol. All words were one

once the massiveness of the cow
was how she loved this world; and longed for more

The slender habitual vision of cow
penetrates the smoke, the misty mourning
of butchers who stand waiting wearing
leather aprons holding in their hands bone-
handled knives — the sharper the edge
the grimmer the glitter.

ARTICULATION

Beginning (articulus)

Art. Article. Articulate. Artifact. Artery. Arthritic.
Arthropod. All about joints, where the pieces
connect. Also called mereology, this thinking
about the pieces as the puzzle puzzles: is
a thing the part of the thing, is everything
part of itself, are two distinct things never
part of each other. The wax and the candle
are part of each other. The wax wanes
into light and smoke, the candle wavers
shadowing itself onto the wall of the room
in which the thinker is part of the darkness.

He was when he was a boy able to think
and would. If he could again.

Begin Again

Modern ontologists and metaphysicians unite;
be part and parcel of; see part. "Pass the Parcel"
is a children's game a boy could play in which
a parcel's passed while music plays. The holder
when the music stops unwraps a layer. A grand
geology builds, subtracts.

partire, partiri "divide, share"

"I draw a rabbit that to you looks like a duck.
Have I thereby made two drawings? I write 'p'
on my office glass door; from the outside you read 'q.'
Have I therefore produced two letter-tokens?

And what if Mary joins you and reads it upside down:
have I also written the letter 'b'?

Surely then I have also written the letter 'd,'
as my upside-down office-mate John points out.
This multiplication of entities seems preposterous.
There is just one thing there, one inscription,
and what it looks (or means) to you or me
or Mary or John is totally irrelevant to what that thing is.
(Varzi 2008)" http://seop.leeds.ac.uk/entries/mereology/

The translucent skin of the onion keeps
pushing itself outward, enraptured,
a wrapping opening onto its core — a mind of onion.

Finally Beginning

We begin. No, we don't. We hover over choices, claiming and
proclaiming one thing as beginning
then another. His child's illness, the illness

"devastating" in all the texts
Devastate   vast   waste

Large windy areas, surfaces.
He travels such spaces, walks
across plains marked with grids, go boards,
lines and intersections bewildering
but full of fate. Nineteen squared.

(He is, it happens, crossing a country on his way
somewhere, and below him is desert and from

80

his window he can see roads,
miles and more of lines, dramatic
intersections, and at another distance circles
irrigation, and it is uncertain that he looks, sees
and notes this landscape. But he would notice,
or should, a cloud beneath him brilliant in sun
with serrated edges a sort of lesson in something
and beneath that the black shadow of cloud also
fingered intricately along its edges, also taking
slightly altering shapes omens the process of evaporation
and the air cooling along the edges of cloud
the land below parched, piercingly
bright in sun.) Shadow is mere delusion.
Light lessened. Mere, pure. Mereology. A study
of the relationship of parts to parts,
to a whole, but there is no whole.

So he began, or thought he began, his crossing as if
he were making a choice and his choice felt new and
felt full yet light, as of weight and also of visibility.
Lightness was his choice, to live a life or be a young
man full of light and without regard for the shadow
following him into the source. His lungs full of light,
enough to keep him, to enliven him. All he did was leave
home and go to school, what millions do and have done.
And school was not enlightening, but the after times —
Chimes Street, a bewilderment of girls
and garrulousness he discovered, uncovered
in his light his dark engagements.
A place where the war hence Authority
was condemned hence his lightness, fatally implied.
Fellows, followers against folly. Parts rejecting the whole,
which is how it happens, some beginnings.
The white light against war was our desire,

or desire was the filament which glowed against
the current war. The current then-war was not
like the current now-war, or it was and is,
and there has been always always war and
the young men gathered on Chimes Street
were expected to go and some to come back
and some not, and some parts of some to remain
there in the jungles or deserts or streets where war was.
And so some years passed and he did not go,
he lengthened his error he remained. A fact.

"Fact" from the Latin *factum*, a noun derived
from *facere*, to make. He began
to make his facts. This was a beginning.
The tedious gathering of the facts of others or
the energetic production of one's own as in how
scientific facts are the result of the instruments
used to produce them? Is that a fact?

Psalm 119: I am Thine, save me;
for I have sought Thy precepts.

Another man another meaning. She began
to wish it so, and so engaged
a gathering in the scifi parallel
in which a child thrives as
twin to the real one — a death on one side
of symmetry balanced by the possible elsewhere.
Any twin invokes a version a fantasy. The child
in his illness is doubled, one version
part of the time, the other other
but there is no other there is only one ever
a child a cure and a consolation to his parents no

other than articulation of the need the narrowing
possibility as when the contrail glints pink
against the going of the sun and the little family joins
hands to watch and consider it the world

making itself a drama act three closing curtain
of particulate matter the grit engaging the photons
and then the swelling applause it happens
to be all over and we thought we were about
to start.

Rex noster promptus est   Our king is swift
Suscipere sanguinem innocentum   to receive the blood of innocents
Sed nubes super eundem sanguinem   But over the same blood clouds
plangunt.   are grieving.

Hildegard of Bingen

A cloud of the possible
surrounds every non-thing
and will clear a path a passage forward
or the appearance of it. Disappearance
breeds all possibility. *Weolcan*, ME for cloud,
replaced by *clud*, clod, clot, cloud.
The weather clears like a mind, a word
            erased: *explicit.*

CLOUDLESS

Modeled from dust, the world fears the wind
Edmond Jabès

And I will make the rivers dry, and sell the land into the hand of
the wicked
Ezekiel 30:12

SAYINGS OF THE DESERT FATHERS

(after the translations by Benedicta Ward, SLG, and others)

The Dark as Memorial to Light

"While the ship is at sea, it consumes itself like a candle, prey to dangers of wind and of wave. When it reaches harbor, it no longer shines on its own calamities, waves or winds. While you are among men you must waste yourself in bright defenses. But when you reach the harbor of silence, you have no need for burning."

The Scribe Who Would Eat No Bread

One came begging him to copy a book. He copied leaving out phrases, leaving out punctuation. One said, "There are words missing." He said, "Read the ones you have then come back for more."

Truly, I have seen monks fleeing, leaving their white-washed cells and also their parchments, and they did not close the doors, but left leaving doors open.

Some said of him that he had a furrow in his chest from the tears that fell all his life while he sat at his work. When they learned that he was dead, they said, weeping, "Truly you are blessed, for you wept for yourself in this world! He who does not weep for himself now will weep eternally; it is impossible not to weep, either now or in memory."

A Form of Greed, or Gratitude

It was also said of him that on Saturday evenings, preparing for the glory of Sunday, he would turn his back on the sun and stretch out his hands towards the east until once again the sun shone on his face. Then he would sit down.

Who receives something from another because of his poverty or his need has therein his reward, and because he is ashamed, when he repays it he does so in secret. But it is the opposite for the mad; they receive in secret, but repay in the presence of the angels, the archangels and the righteous.

Toward a Name for All and None

Another time when he was living with disciples on the borders of Persia two of the others went hunting. They spread nets around an area of forty miles or more, to kill everything within the nets. Seeing him all hairy and looking like a wild man they said, "Tell us if you are a man or a ghost. Tell us if you are Orion." He said, "I am a man who has come away to weep for his sins." They said to him "There is no god save the sun, the fire, and the water, which we worship." He said to them, "There is no god save the wind, the mint, and the fishes, which we worship." And they said to him "There is no god save the torments, the tortures, and the terrors, which all fear." And he said to them "There is no god save the totality, and the indifference, and the denigration, which no one escapes."

In the Realms of the Pronouns

While traveling through a certain region, he saw one whom someone had seized believing he had killed another. He went and questioned him. Learning that he had been wrongly accused, he said to those holding him, "Where is the dead man?" They showed him to him. Telling them to pray, he went to him. Stretching his hand toward heaven, he stood up. He said to him in front of them, "Tell us who killed you." He said, "As I was going into the church I gave that one alms. He killed me, then he threw me into the vestry. Therefore I beseech you to take the money and give it to my heirs." Then he said to him "Go and rest until one comes to waken you."

If a Man Cannot Understand My Silence, He Will Never Understand My Words
                              Anthony of Sourozh

John Tavener under the influence of Metropolitan Anthony of Sourozh composed many sounds to shatter silence including the all-night vigil the seven-hour-long The Veil of The Temple. Voices voices.

The Dead Remain Dead

The first one, leaving his own dead, went to weep over the other's; this was how he served his necessary god, with intentions elegant and full of sweetness. It was said, for instance, of one that he killed a basilisk. Going into the desert for water he saw a basilisk, upon which seeing he threw himself eyes down into the sand saying, "Either I die or he does," upon which speaking the basilisk burst into silent flames.

About the Measure of Abstinence

In food and drink, they said, one should partake in a measure somewhat less than one's actual need, that is, not to fill the stomach completely. One should establish a measure for oneself, whether in cooked food or in wine. The measure of abstinence is not limited to food and drink but embraces also conversations, sleep, garments, poetry, passion and all the senses. Each of these should have its own measure of abstinence.

How to establish a measure of food and drink, at less than one's need? Take away one ounce from the total quantity of bread and other foods. As regards water and wine taken together, take away less than half a cup. It would be well to drink only once a day; if you must, drink twice a day, but each time less than you need. When thoughts are troubled, the quantity of food and drink should be reduced; food by another ounce and all drink by a cup, so that in all food is reduced by two ounces and drink by one cup.

The Measure of Weeping

"While we have time, let us learn to be silent. Be dead in relation to every one, and you will find peace. I speak here touching thoughts, touching all kinds of activities, relationships with men, women, dogs, cats and cares."

"Do you wish to be free of afflictions and not to be burdened by them? Expect greater ones, and you will find peace."

"Who allows himself to be evil and the cause of evils disagrees with no one, quarrels with no one, is not wroth with anyone, but considers every man better and wiser than himself."

The Nature of Fame

He questioned him, saying "If I go away to weep for my sins, how should I live?" And he said "If you live somewhere, do not seek to be known for anything special; do not say, for example, I do not go to the agora; or perhaps, I do not eat grapes, for these things make an empty reputation and later you will be sorry, for men rush to where they find these practices." He said to him "Then what shall I do?" He said "Wherever you live, follow the same manner of life as everyone else, and if you see peaceful ones do the same and you will be at peace. For this is humility, to see yourself to be the same as the rest. When they see you do not go beyond limits, they will consider you to be the same as everyone and no one will trouble you."

A Purging of the Fellow-Feeling

In every desert there grow two plants, called (in these corrupt days) *spurge* and *purslane*. They are sisters of the soil. The one cures, the other kills; or, they both kill, they both cure. They grow in broad patterns, intricate as weavings of the desert peoples. One is the shadow, one is the shadow.

It happens that we have two of many things, parts of the body to give us company — the ear is the ear's dear companion, the hand the hand's. So strange then the loneliness of the genital, the heart.

Kaaba or The Orient

Qibla, the sacred direction (orientation)
the body lies in its grave on its side, facing the qibla.

So We Must Reinvent Forgetting

The young and the old are frightened by orphans
but middle age is intrigued — the orphan is everywhere
at home, unhindered. And the orphan finds,
everywhere, something

every thing is an orphan

*can we imagine that the Eden serpent and the dove of the holy spirit
are first cousins*   Peter Greenaway

Vector, Arrow, Carrier

A scalar field has only one attribute: for instance, ink on a page.
The temperature of a room. But wind is non-scalar — velocity
and direction. But also temperature, and color, and cause, and
consequence. A candle flame vector-like in shape and color.

Humility

Theophrastus replaced Aristotle as head of the Academy. Who
replaced Theophrastus?

The Ground Itself, Humus

Humility collects the soul into a single point by the power of silence
(Isaac of Ninevah) *a truly humble being wishes to form himself into*
himself, to become nothing as if he had never been born. When he is
completely hidden to himself within himself he is god.

It is One's duty to erase himself completely. To joyfully find the most
efficient path through all points of the space into which he is born
to erase those points — space-filling curves which pass through every
point of the region of his life. To pierce, penetrate, clarify.

Erasure of Aristotle. Erase also the Academy. Mutation alteration
defacement and disappearance, a new verb *disappear* appeared in
the papers about that time, the American secrecy a boy believes he is
riding the shoulders of a giant of the world his father they float alone
a whiteness of crushed seashell a road they witness the night the
path between home and not home the heavy bearing of a boy's father
ridden by ghastly memory then the sound of feet one then another
are real a rising of reality into the path the paradoxical dark the
danger fathers arising with the moon a shadow cast cost of shadows
lost a rising like new moon

event and its further form eventual
even and evening.

Those who suffer the need for things must against their very will
amass mere things — "sometimes I need stuff" he said against tears,
tearing of his home apart the walls he had made of journals stacked;

I do not see the bird in the grape vine
I do not touch the bird in the grape vine
but I see his shadow as sunlight burns
greenly through the leaf
I hear his voice violate the heart the heat of the air.

MOUNTAIN FOLDS, VALLEY FOLDS

A paper rose revealed my hand
creased but readable in my
hand the paper rising into mind I mind
a little the tattering that comes with the season

seizin in law possession to take in hand never
mind the rose rising in my hand according
to instruction accordion pleats
of paper mount

amounting less because the little
land of the hand is my
range my circuitry surrounding

having-in-hand as usual the story of the losses
lessens the need for this class in how
to make out of paper a rose any color
of paper pauper

in forma pauperis they wrote would
write as if to allow the right not to pay
playing back and
forth paper to pauper a game in hand:

remember the reed that flattens to
something to write on some thing foldable
suitable for the pocket the landscape internal

creased and crushed is the land we live on
love the paper forms maps for instance
books of hands and
harrowed flowering.

THE ROMANCE OF THE SEA

A group of words deflect, reflect in darkening
water as evening enters and the ship
sails in — the words matter, but are
unreadable the surface bends of
water bends and sends light scattering colors
of letters; imagine it, imagine it as
reproducible somewhere has been done
before to death — harbor, light, evening,
reflections. A name a nationality. Boats get named.
The evening reflection on water — the water
oily and of its own color, of the color of refracted light against the
molecules, a grating
of light against a surface contain — these words
unreadable. Second Wind
is the number one name of sailboats,
but this engine muffled by water
has no use for wind or readers,
is all business, all surface water wavery will...
five names for one tanker since it was known
notoriously, currently Dong Fang Ocean...
ship type: dry cargo. No liquids
allowed. Ex Exxon.

THE NARRATIVE IMPULSE—
NORTH AND SOUTH

Miraculous Brutality

The story of Our Lady of Guadalupe is of stars
on her robe; as her children climbed the mountain
Coatlicue gave birth. Huitzilopochtli
was born killing his four-hundred-
twenty-one brothers as the brothers
died Huitzilopochtli threw their bodies into
space where they became the stars of our universe.

Drops of blood fell onto the earth to become
flowers—roses, some of them, pretty in winter
on the mountainside, also portulaca passing
through the small gate, the strait passage
of mortality, and purslane and porcelain,
feathered petals and pork and parsley
and all the pretty things of new worlds.

Portulaca, Small Gate

In nature all functions are continuous
as for instance height graphed against age
of a flower or depth of snow or despair
against the time of night the hours passing
when roses do not grow so ordinary in Mexico.

Sound is Continuous in the Ear

What is being mimicked when we hear
recorded music? when we hear it
from single-source personal machinery
as we walk in the night toward home
in winter with wind blocked from the ear

but not the face, the scarf elegant and
useful printed with roses our lady's
gift and stars

to us presents of peril the perilous
universe a single turning a line of verse continuous.
Let us call on the citizens for help.

Question What is the sign that a man has attained to purity of
heart, and when does a woman know that his heart has entered
into purity?

Answer When he sees all men as good and no woman appears to
him to be defiled, then in very truth is his heart pure. For how could
anyone fulfill the word of the Apostle, that "A man should esteem
all better than himself" with a sincere heart, if he does not attain to
the saying, "Only a blinded eye sees itself"? (Isaac the Syrian, I 37)

Every saint like every candle consumes itself wholly, to die into a
puff of soot—wax and wick lose equally every race. Thus a failure to
be relished, proud oblivion: a greatest lower bound.

The Eye Is a Kind of Candle and

tears are an imperfection of combustion. Yet the eye receives light,
the candle sheds; the eye has nothing to shed but tears, a cause in
itself for crying.

97

AT HENRI MICHAUX'S

I told him how much I envied him for this
silence. He interrupted me: From time to time I hear
a child. That's normal, I said to him without thinking.
Excuse me, he cut me off once again, it's not at all
normal. It would be normal if I heard a tiger, not a child.
        Mircea Eliade, *Journal II*, 21 July 1961

To celebrate sound and silence we have
fabulous friends and fable is a sound especially
at night with light reflecting off the page.

They do sleep some nights and hear only
distantly the cries tigerish of territory.
If I cry myself I show sincerity
of the child not the tiger. Sincere tiger
startles. I sleep soundly
through silence but awaken with a start.

        ...

Geometry meant measure
of the earth itself not distant silence
before flayed earth naked turned

abstract as any continuous curve
as in words *stretched*: tense, tendon,
tenet, tent, tenor, tender, pretend
all that in space extended
hypotenuse tenure in time, too. Sounds
of a child in the night is natural

a cry having lost his toy her toy
a stuffed tiger a doll a dearness
under duress. This in the night

        ...

under the linens a lining
so-called "bed-clothes" in which to wrap
and sleep a self a me

involved: the circling sounds
or lines out of sight I thought
I heard the told the telling
driving north to south entire
continental the words wore
out, no, driving Prudhoe Bay

to Ushuaia (the terminus
was Buenos Aires when as a child
I heard first the story of the highway

some engineer's dream) Line lingers
lingery lingerie, but I meant
a dream of driving whole continents
contiguous continuously
toying out the time.
A dream is dreary a drive

in the night with tigers passing
jungled beyond the windows
the cheering sounds of sounds of

celebrate that. Earth. I live here.
I am abstract. Outrageous.
I cry and cringe. Tiger and Toy. Child.

A QUESTIONING (MARGERY KEMPE)

Another time a great cleric came to her asking
how these words should be understood: *Crescite
et multiplicamini*
to which others had answered Patience
is more worthy than Persistence — but no,
she said it is not so.

My body is not that body, Mine is my own
agreement/argument with itself, with its future.
Yours is yours, a shining a burning, do not
annoy the past with your persistence, pastoral.

Increase. Multiply. The beasts do their part, one
into two, into four, into eight, into sixteen.
And the fear of you and the dread of you shall be
upon every beast of the earth to your shame, and
upon every fowl of the air, upon all that moveth
upon the earth, and upon all the fishes
the dread of your hand...

And I will require your blood for their lives
at the hand of God I will require it and then
Margery Kempe stopped speaking, trembling
with a hunger without shame, she read
*et terror vester ac tremor sit super cuncta animalia
terrae et super omnes volucres caeli cum universis
quae moventur in terra omnes pisces maris manui
vestrae traditi sunt*

IN A FAMILIAR FORM

Question What are the exact tokens and accurate signs that the fruit which is hidden in the soul has begun to appear from one's mad labor?

Answer The gift of abundant tears which come without effort. For tears are a boundary between what is bodily and what is spiritual and between passion and purity...one begins to shed the various skins of the present age and crosses back and forth the boundary, a shuttle collecting the threads, unraveling (un traveling) that which lies inside visible nature... by reason of this constant converse with tears one imbibes words with his food and drink....

There are tears that burn and there are tears that anoint as with oil. All tears that flow out of contrition and anguish of heart dry up and burn the body, and often even the governing faculty feels the injury caused by their outflow. At first she must necessarily come to this order of tears and through them the door is opened to enter into the second order, which is superior to the first; this is the realm wherein you offer yourself mercy.

Among the mad, the made
minds, the minds' made up
image, the mind an imaginary study,
a science not soothing, soothless, slothful.

These are tears shed because of insight; they make the body beautiful and anoint it as if with oil. They anoint the body but they also offer a faceless fear full of future. — *contra* St Isaac of Ninevah, now Mosul

MARGERY KEMPE AND THE QUESTIONINGS

Later a lesser cleric came to her to ask what words
she would recommend for one so humble, so pointless.

She replied: mine is not the body, my disagreeable need. Persist
at risk. Do as you will.

He said: Too many words. I am small and all.

She said: Increase, multiply. The smallness of one
becomes two, then four, eight, sixteen, thirty-
two of you

and the fear of you and the dread of you shall be upon every
beast — your pets will tremble,
your livestock will flee — and neither air nor water
will hide them. Into your well-toothed mouth
they will scamper

and your anguish will require their blood.

And then Margery Kempe stopped speaking
to the lesser cleric with a shameful hunger

who had no Latin, no Greek, no books.
"Banish" is a curious word. To summon. To curse.

BEAUTIFUL ISLAND:

"night was paper and we were ink"
    —Adonis

There air is a kind of liveliness, otherwise dense with necessity

if the sounds in the air are

if I wash myself with snow water, and make my hands
never so clean (Job 9:30).   "Resuming their journey through
another pass to the south they came to the beautiful lake of
Tsui-sia-hia, or lake of the Water Savages, a distinct tribe who
live on its banks. They are a degraded race, and are employed
as slaves by the Chinese"

night was paper and we were ink

night was figure and light was ground

night was ink and light was paper

"they tattoo their faces in bands across the nose,
are tall, and would be well-proportioned but for
a pernicious habit they indulge in of tying cloths
tightly round their waists, which deforms them
very much"   ("On a Journey through Formosa
from Tamsui to Taiwanfu." *The Geographical
Magazine* 4, 1877)
night was paper and light was ink

Abba Moses said to him, "Go and sit in your cell
and your cell will teach you everything"

night was night and light was light

at war with the universe
my country was losing and I was
at war with my country and I was lost
night was fear and light was fear

night was day and light was night

"Navigating lagoons during gales" (an engraving
from the hand of Hornby Grimani in *The Illustrated
London News*, 1890) and there were water buffalo
pursuing; also Mr. Grimani's recollection sketched
with drama rewarding the accurate eye the hand
made miraculous — feet of a boy, head of a dragon

Abba Nilus said, "The arrows of the enemy
cannot touch one who loves quietness; but he
who moves about in a crowd will often be wounded"

Theophilus, Bishop of Alexandria: "If he does not learn from my
silence, neither will he learn from my words"

When I kept silence, my bones waxed old
through my roaring all the day long (Psalm 32:3)

a muddle of words words words:
servus, slave — observe, serve, deserve.
We do think this way: attend, stretch

toward — be there be there, serve,
observe, attend, serve well (well enough)

I cannot well repeat how there I entered,   So full was I
of slumber at the moment   In which I had abandoned
the true way, he said. Longfellow said.

I read that one, and *Hiawatha* and *Evangeline*,
because they were an honorable reading,
full of a grandeur of a past we did aspire

a shock it is to find you have a past
not the one you remember. Forgone, forgotten.

AN UNSAYING

History Is A Word for Fear, to Fear

Walk in fear of All to feel no fear. He with the fear of All
within him wears the invincible armor of ignorance. This makes
him strong and able to take on anything, even things which
are impossible. Such a one is a giant surrounded by monkeys, or a
roaring lion among foxes. He goes forward trusting in all and his
ability to strike and paralyze his foes. He wields the blazing club
of ignorance, of wisdom. — *c.f.* St. Symeon the New Theologian,
his "The Practical and Theological Chapters"

When we lay bare the hidden meaning of history, writing is seen
to teach that the birth which distresses the tyrant is the beginning
of the literary life. — *against* St. Gregory of Nyssa, *The Life of
Letters*

Study Much and Remember Little

O strange and inconceivable thing! We did not really die, we
were not really buried, we were not really crucified and raised
again, our imitation was but a figure, while our failure is a reality.
All who are not literary were actually crucified, and actually
buried, and truly rose again... I, without suffering or toil, or the
fellowship of pain, I am called to the real again. — in memory of
St. Cyril of Jerusalem, *On those Who Learn Written Language*

He who knows anything knows everything. Or, he who is dead is
alive only to himself. — *after* St. John Climacus

Repentance is a contract with all who live for a second life. A
penitent buys his own humility. Repentance is constant distrust
of the body. Repentance is self-condemning reflection,

and carefree self-care. Repentance is the daughter of hope and the renunciation of despair. A penitent is a graceful convict. Reentance is reconciliation with the Author by the practice of good deeds contrary to the book. Repentance is purification of vocabulary. Repentance is the voluntary enduring of story. A penitent inflicts his own narrative. Repentance is a mighty persecution of the flesh, and a striking of the soul into vigorous awareness. —*contra* St. John Climacus

Natura Naturans as Sin Sinning

Those who seek humility should bear in mind the three following things: that they are the worst of sinners, that they are the most despicable of all creatures since their state is an unnatural one, and that they are even more pitiable than the demons, since they are slaves to the demon of literacy.

You will also profit if you say this to yourself: how do I know what (or how many) other people's sins are, or whether they are greater than or equal to my own? In our ignorance you and I, My Soul My Self, are worse than all others, we are dust and ashes under their feet. How can I not regard myself as more despicable than all other creatures, for they act in accordance with the nature they have been given, while I, owing to my literacy, am in a state contrary to nature. —the logic of St. Gregory of Sinai, *Philokalia.*

Listen, a scraping of the page against page, obliteration:
Nothing left to read or reason.

Individual poems appeared in the following journals:

viz.interarts (UCSC): "Continuous Computation"
Octopus: "Cloud (Continued)," "Living in Weather,"
   "Explicit by the Bedside"
New American Writing: "Sayings of the Desert Fathers"
Fence: "Articulation"
A Public Space: "Crystalline Structure, Threat of Weather"
Chronicle of Higher Education: "Cloud as an Open Set Maps
   onto the Hillside"
Diode: "We Who Live Here See Air," "Cipher," "At Henri
   Michaux's," "Margery Kempe and the Questionings"
THE ARCADIA PROJECT: "A Measured Narrowness"

≈

"Sayings of the Desert Fathers," and "An Unsaying" are after (with
distortions) the sayings of Abraham, Amones, Barsanuphius, John
Cassian, Miletius, Motius, Poemen-called-The-Shepherd, and
Megethius: translations by Benedicta Ward, SLG, and others.
Thanks to Nic Ramke for bringing these source texts to my attention,
and for reading the resulting poems with care and concern.

≈

"In a Familiar Form" is a reworking/rewording of parts of *The
Ascetical Homilies of Saint Isaac the Syrian,* translated by the Holy
Transfiguration Monastery, Boston, 1984.

Bin Ramke, author of *Theory of Mind: New and Selected Poems* (Omnidawn, 2009), edits the Denver Quarterly and teaches writing at the University of Denver and also teaches at the Art Institute of Chicago. He grew up on the Gulf coast and for twenty years edited a poetry series for a southern university press. He won the Yale Younger Poets Award in 1978. This is his eleventh book.

Aerial
by Bin Ramke

Cover text set in Castellar MT Std and Electra LT Std.
Interior text set in Electra LT Std.

Cover art by Jan Aronson,
"Cloud Triptych #42"

Cover and interior design by Cassandra Smith

Omnidawn Publishing
Richmond, California
2012

Ken Keegan & Rusty Morrison, Co-Publishers & Senior Editors
Cassandra Smith, Poetry Editor & Book Designer
Gillian Hamel, Poetry Editor & OmniVerse Managing Editor
Sara Mumolo, Poetry Editor & OmniVerse New-Work Editor
Peter Burghardt, Poetry Editor & Bookstore Outreach Manager
Jared Alford, Facebook Editor
Juliana Paslay, Bookstore Outreach & Features Writer
Turner Canty, Features Writer
Craig Santos Perez, Media Consultant